WRESTLING SUPERST★RS

RANDY ORTON

BY JESSE ARMSTRONG

BELLWETHER MEDIA • MINNEAPOLIS, MN

EPIC BOOKS are no ordinary books. They burst with intense action, high-speed heroics, and shadows of the unknown. Are you ready for an Epic adventure?

This edition first published in 2015 by Bellwether Media, Inc.

No part of this publication may be reproduced in whole or in part without written permission of the publisher. For information regarding permission, write to Bellwether Media, Inc., Attention: Permissions Department, 5357 Penn Avenue South, Minneapolis, MN 55419.

Library of Congress Cataloging-in-Publication Data

Armstrong, Jesse.
  Randy Orton / by Jesse Armstrong.
    pages cm. – (Epic. Wrestling Superstars)
  Includes bibliographical references and index.
  Summary: "Engaging images accompany information about Randy Orton. The combination of high-interest subject matter and light text is intended for students in grades 2 through 7"– Provided by publisher.
  Audience: Ages 7-12.
  ISBN 978-1-62617-182-4 (hardcover : alk. paper)
  1. Orton, Randy–Juvenile literature. 2. Wrestlers–United States–Biography–Juvenile literature. I. Title.
  GV1196.O77A76 2015
  796.812092–dc23
  [B]
                              2014040637

Printed in the United States of America, North Mankato, MN.

TABLE OF CONTENTS

WARNING!

The wrestling moves used in this book are performed by professionals.
Do not attempt to reenact any of the moves performed in this book.

THE DEBUT

Randy Orton enters the ring for his tryout match. He is ready to become a third generation wrestler. Hardcore Holly waits to take him on.

Holly beats on Orton. But Orton battles back. Eventually he flies from the top ropes onto Holly. Then he traps Holly for a **three count**. Orton sends a strong message in his **debut**.

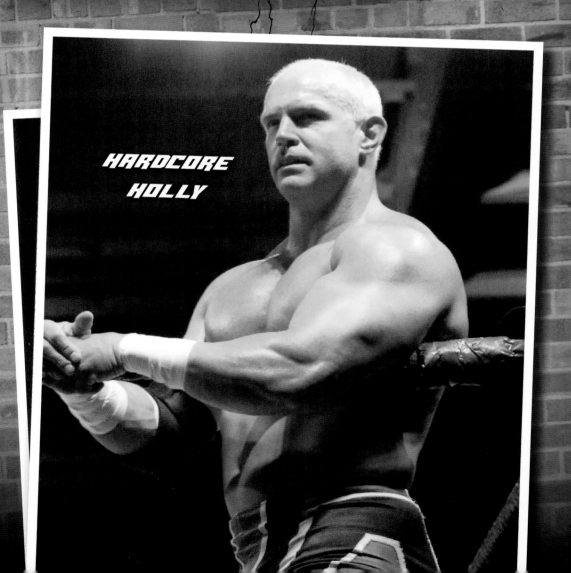

HARDCORE HOLLY

WHO IS RANDY ORTON?

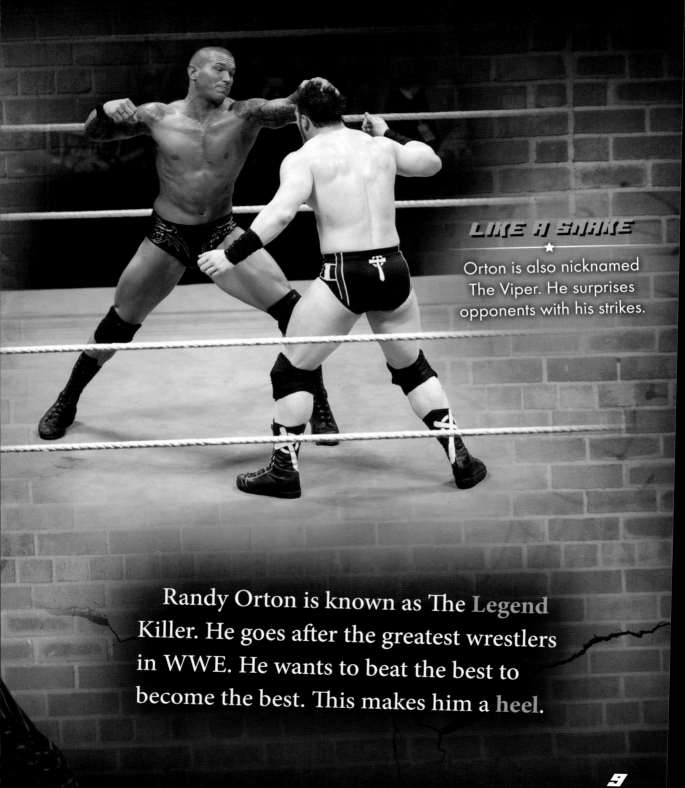

Randy Orton is known as The Legend Killer. He goes after the greatest wrestlers in WWE. He wants to beat the best to become the best. This makes him a heel.

LIFE BEFORE WWE

BRET THE BABYSITTER

★

Superstar Bret Hart sometimes watched 5-year-old Randy backstage.

"COWBOY" BOB ORTON

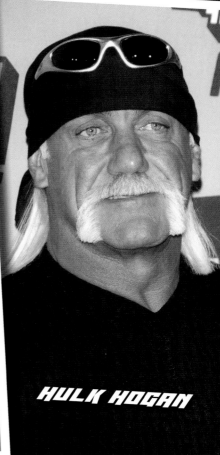

HULK HOGAN

Orton grew up around wrestlers. His dad was "Cowboy" Bob Orton. His uncle and grandpa also wrestled. Hulk Hogan and other stars would stop by his family home.

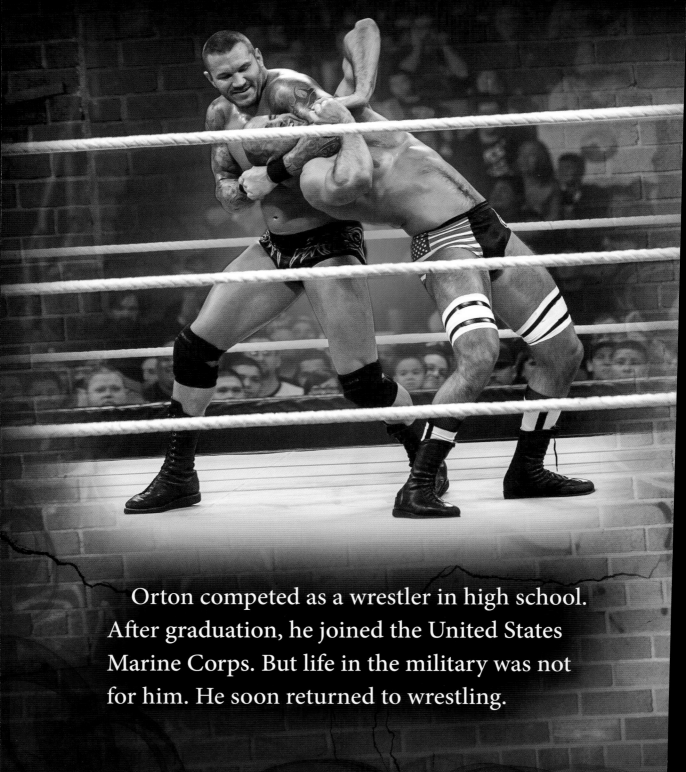

Orton competed as a wrestler in high school. After graduation, he joined the United States Marine Corps. But life in the military was not for him. He soon returned to wrestling.

Orton has acted in movies.
He especially enjoyed
his stunt work in
12 Rounds 2: Reloaded.

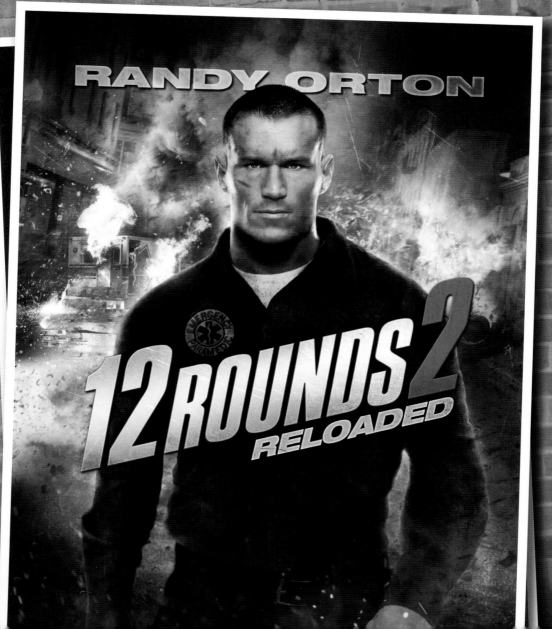

A WWE SUPERSTAR

STAR PROFILE

WRESTLING NAME:	Randy Orton
REAL NAME:	Randy Keith Orton
BIRTHDATE:	April 1, 1980
HOMETOWN:	St. Louis, Missouri
HEIGHT:	6 feet, 5 inches (2 meters)
WEIGHT:	235 pounds (107 kilograms)
WWE DEBUT:	2002
FINISHING MOVE:	RKO

WWE gave Orton a developmental contract in 2001. By 2003, he earned his first title. The championship made him hungry for more wins.

Orton has since collected more than ten titles. He has defeated John Cena and Triple H to claim a few of those.

TRIPLE H

JOHN CENA

WINNING MOVES

RKO

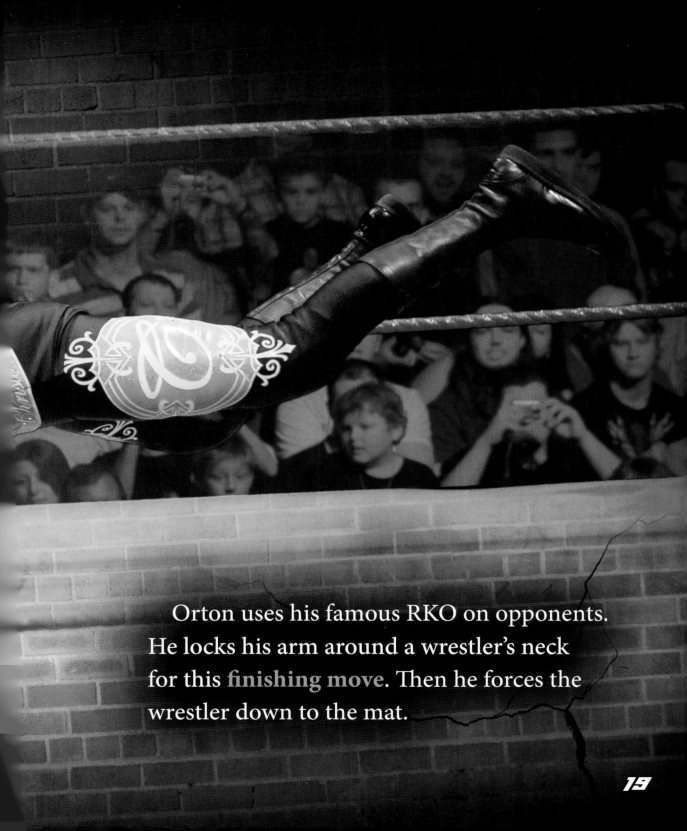

Orton uses his famous RKO on opponents. He locks his arm around a wrestler's neck for this **finishing move**. Then he forces the wrestler down to the mat.

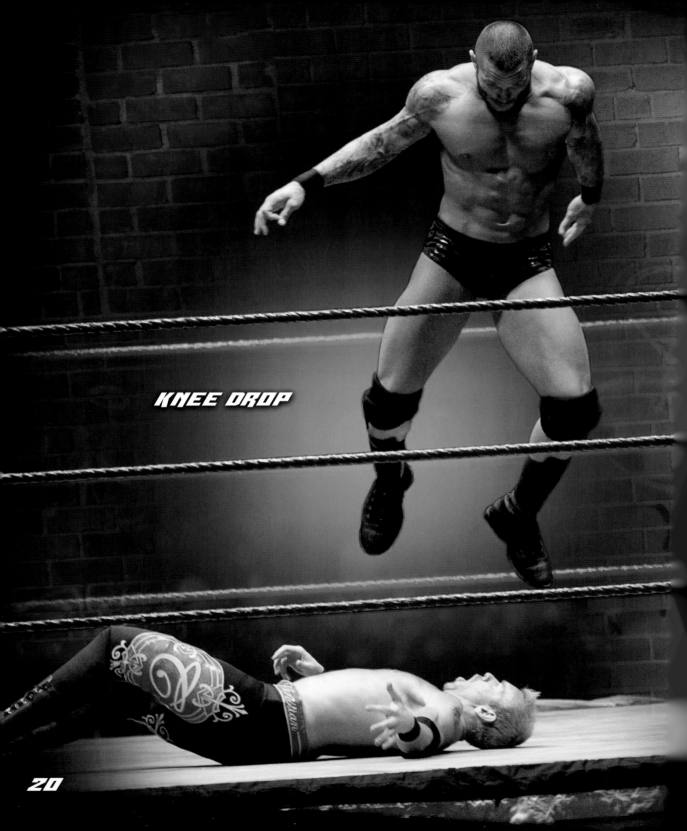

KNEE DROP

Another signature move is a hit called the Knee Drop. Orton jumps high into the air. Then he drives his knee into his opponent!

GLOSSARY

debut—first official appearance

developmental contract—an agreement between WWE and a wrestler; WWE promises to train the wrestler in smaller leagues.

finishing move—a wrestling move that finishes off an opponent

hardcore—fierce

heel—a wrestler viewed as a villain

legend—a star who has lasting fame

signature move—a move that a wrestler is famous for performing

third generation—following the same path as a parent and grandparent

three count—when a referee counts to three during a pin; this declares a winner.

title—championship

tryout match—a match that offers an unknown wrestler the chance to show his skills

TO LEARN MORE

At the Library

Armstrong, Jesse. *Kofi Kingston*. Minneapolis, Minn.: Bellwether Media, 2015.

Black, Jake. *WWE General Manager's Handbook*. New York, N.Y.: Grosset & Dunlap, 2012.

West, Tracey. *Race to the Rumble*. New York, N.Y.: Grosset & Dunlap, 2011.

On the Web

Learning more about Randy Orton is as easy as 1, 2, 3.

1. Go to www.factsurfer.com.

2. Enter "Randy Orton" into the search box.

3. Click the "Surf" button and you will see a list of related web sites.

With factsurfer.com, finding more information is just a click away.

INDEX